The Specific Learning Difficulties Profile and associated conditions

by Jan Poustie

This book, part of the Identification Solutions for Specific Learning Difficulties Library, is dedicated to my lovely daughter Briony without whom it would never have been written.

Contents

This book has been written to help both professionals and non-professionals find out the reasons why some individuals are failing to succeed, and to provide information on where to turn for help in overcoming their difficulties.

The pages of this book have been laid out with irregular right-hand margins and without unnecessary hyphenation to aid those with visual difficulties.

Acknowledgements

The Identification Solutions for Specific Learning Difficulties Library has only been made possible through the cooperation of many agencies and professionals to whom I am greatly indebted. The generosity of my colleagues has been exceptional. They have given their time (a precious commodity for all of them) plus their advice and the benefit of their expertise. All of the conditions within the Specific Learning Difficulties Profile are medically based. Therefore a library of this type could not be written without a great deal of input from the medical profession. Many grateful thanks go to the following educational and medical specialists:

Keith Holland, Behavioural Optometrist

Dr Ian McKinlay, Senior lecturer in Community Child Health, Royal Manchester Children's Hospital

Rosemary Sassoon, Specialist in the educational and medical aspects of handwriting

Dr Peter Gardner, Chartered Educational psychologist and co-founder of Appleford School

Dr Josephine Marriage, Paediatric Audiological Scientist

Christine Stache, Head Occupational Therapist, Musgrove Park Hospital, Taunton

Michèle Lee, Chartered Physiotherapist in paediatrics

Dr Pullaperuma, Consultant Paediatrician with an interest in children with autistic spectrum disorder, Musgrove Park Hospital, Taunton

Veronica M. Connery, Speech and Language Therapist

Denise Caferelli-Dees, Senior Clinical Research Specialist Cochlear (UK) Ltd.

Mary Nash-Wortham, Speech therapist

Dr Hamstra-Bletz, Social scientist

Madeleine Portwood, Specialist Senior Educational Psychologist

Patricia Clayton, Irlen Diagnostician

Dr Christopher Green, Specialist Paediatrician, Head of Child Development Unit, Royal Alexandra Hospital for Children, Sydney, Australia and clinical lecturer at the University of Sidney

Eamon McCrory, Institute of Cognitive Neuroscience, London

Dr Ginny Stacey, Support Tutor for Dyslexic Students at Oxford Brookes University

Violet Brand, International speaker on dyslexia

Professor Rod Nicolson, University of Sheffield

Dr Crispin Bennett, Biochemist

Dr David Horrobin, Research Scientist

Neil Ward, Senior lecturer in analytical and environmental chemistry, University of Surrey

Dr Udo Erasmus, Nutritionist

Many thanks also go to the staff of Taunton reference library, whose helpfulness and keen research skills have made the accessing of information so much easier for me.

iv Acknowledgements

One cannot forget all the others who have helped in the writing of this book, thus making it a richer source of information:

▸ The children (and their parents) and the adults that I work with from whom I have learnt so much.

▸ Teachers and other professionals who have provided information and shared experiences with me.

▸ Members of the Internet SENCO-forum group.

Thanks also go to the many others who have pointed me in the right direction to find essential information.

Alex Richardson, Senior Research Fellow in Neuroscience, Imperial College School of Medicine, University Laboratory of Physiology, Oxford.

John Stein, Professor of Physiology, Oxford University Medical School.

Many thanks also go to the following agencies and organisations, and their staff:

▸ AFASIC (Association For All Speech-Impaired Children)

▸ The Dyspraxia Foundation

▸ The ADHD Family Support Group UK

▸ The Dyslexia Institute

▸ British Dyslexia Association, (and especially to Carol Orton their befriender coordinator)

▸ The College of Speech and Language Therapists

▸ The Handwriting Interest Group

▸ Various departments/members of OFSTED

▸ The Department for Education and Skills

▸ Special Educational Needs Tribunal

▸ Schools Curriculum and Assessment Authority

▸ National Association for Gifted Children

▸ Action for ME

▸ The Hyperactive Children's Support Group UK

▸ Food Standards Agency

Also many thanks to friends and colleagues who supported and encouraged me along the way. Special thanks goes to those who helped, supported and encouraged me during the early years of my learning about specific learning difficulties; namely:

Mary Coyle, Hilary Finn and Stephanie Smith: they were not only my companions at many a conference and lecture but were also generous in their advice.

Hugh Bellamy, Deputy Headteacher, West Somerset Community College. Hugh allowed me freedom to read his many books, and the benefit of his knowledge, opening my eyes to wider horizons.

It was a huge struggle to produce the first edition of this book and it would never have reached the printing stage without my friend Pam Brooks. Never one to be defeated Pam (in a moment of madness) forgot the struggle we had to produce the first edition and gave me one of my best gifts on my 50th birthday - a floppy disk with the new layout of this book on it. My thanks go to both her and her family for supporting me in this endeavour. Finally, thanks to my own family. After six years, they are better able to tolerate the upheaval in their lives that my writing can cause. Thanks to my lovely daughters (for whom I needed to find out the information upon which this book is based). Their acceptance of the need to write so that others can be helped has made my life so much easier. (I delight in the fact that now I get cups of tea made for me, the odd meal cooked and even some help with running the company.)

Jan Poustie

The views expressed by the author are her own and do not necessarily represent those who have contributed to, or assisted with, the writing of this library.

Jan Poustie

Foreword

The Identification Solutions Library will be a valuable resource for parents, teachers and other professionals, as it clearly presents the indicators that can be observed in a range of specific learning difficulties and associated conditions.

Specialists in particular areas have been consulted and their advice, based on knowledge and experience, will certainly increase reader's understanding, making them more aware of the nature of the difficulties they are observing.

There is comprehensive information on where appropriate help, advice and diagnosis can be obtained. This, in itself, will relieve many anxieties – to take a book from a shelf and find a possible solution to problems will, hopefully, ensure that children and adults get the right help at the right time.

Violet Brand

You may find it helpful to have a piece of paper handy to write down the Book/ chapter numbers as you are referred to them.

How to use the Identification Solutions for Specific Learning Difficulties Library

Whilst reading through this library, you may realise that it is likely that you (the parent/adult/professional) and/or your child are affected by the conditions that come within the SpLD Profile. For some of you it might explain much of what has happened in the past and what is happening now, and for some that may seem quite devastating and be a very traumatic experience. If this is the case, it is important to remember that there has been no change in you and/or your child since you picked up the books within this library - just a change in your perception. There is a network of help, support, advice, assessment and intervention available to you which this library will help you to find and access. The information that you gain from the library will not, in itself, fulfil your hopes, dreams and aspirations, but it may be the first step towards their realisation

There are various ways to use this library, all of which involve starting at the Introduction to gain an overview of the Specific Learning Difficulties Profile. After that you can:

➡ Read each book in order.

➡ Start at the book, or chapter within it, which interests you most.

➡ Fill in the checklists in Book 2, and then read the relevant chapters when a checklist indicates that a referral is necessary.

This library has been designed for individuals to 'find' the elements of the picture and then know to whom to go for diagnosis, help and support. Many indicators can be found in more than one condition so you may find yourself being directed to look at several chapters/books within the library if a common indicator is present. It is not the isolated indicator that you need to look for in a condition but the whole picture.

Once you have read all the relevant chapters of the library, you must then decide which of the difficulties is causing the most problems and arrange a referral for that area first, but remember that it can take months before you (or the child/ adult) is seen.

Please do not wait until a diagnosis has been made before contacting your relevant local help and support groups – they exist just for you, whether you are a parent, teenager, adult or professional. (They will not think that you have wasted their time if the diagnosis shows that you or the child/adult does not, after all, have the condition in the end.)

If you wish your identification to be reliable then it is vital that you do not just look at the checklists and/or the index. Instead, you need to go on to look at the relevant chapters as each condition needs to be viewed as a 'whole'. As you are referred from chapter to chapter the picture will emerge. You will usually 'know' when the full picture has emerged as it will 'feel right and complete'. Many who read this library may have one or two of the indicators for a particular condition but this does not necessarily mean that they have this condition. (It's a bit like a sneeze does not mean that you have flu!)

A word from the author

Most of us go to school, maybe we go on to college and possibly then go onto university. At each of these points in our lives certain aspects of our functioning changes and/or become important. Thus the quickly growing teenager finds that s/he can start to literally look down on his/her parents (a source of great delight to the student!) People tend to think of specific learning difficulties in the context of educational situations; e.g. school and college. However, unlike gaining height which has a fixed time frame in which it occurs Specific Learning Difficulties goes on into adulthood. By finding the right job you may not have to face the daily embarrassment caused by poor literacy, behavioural, language, social or mathematical skills but you still have to face the fact that life is much more of a struggle. Many of us who are in this situation struggle silently and (especially if we are professionals) we do not disclose our own learning difficulties for fear of being ridiculed or thought less of professionally. However, if we all continue to do this then few of those who are in a position to help will have a real understanding of our fears for our own children and an understanding of just how far-ranging these conditions are in their effects upon life. I hope that the account of my own life that follows below may act as a catalyst to help others.

When we mention the term Specific Learning Difficulties (SpLD) many presume that we are talking about Dyslexia. Few people realise that there are a range of conditions that come under the SpLD heading and that all of them can be equally as devastating as Dyslexia in their impact upon one's life. Having a range of Specific Learning Difficulties Profile conditions myself has not made writing educational reference books at all easy. As a result of my Attention Deficits, I enjoy doing the research for my books but hate the need for attention to detail that the writing up requires. My Dyspraxia results in frequent visits to an osteopath due to sitting at my computer for far too many hours each day (and night). My Dyscalculia results in me making far too many silly errors when sorting out the page numbering. My word-finding difficulties mean that the desired words elude me at just the wrong moment—yes I know what I want to say but cannot get the right 'feel' across to you, the reader. The net result is a great deal of stress. My writing becomes not only 'all-consuming' but also far too time-consuming. How I envy my sister who in the space of an afternoon can write what I struggle to produce in four days!

Why do I write when for me it is so exhausting, stressful and so time consuming that it takes me away from precious time with my daughters before they grow up and leave this particular nest? The answer is simple. I want the circle to be broken, that vicious circle of failure and frustration in one generation leading to failure and despair in another.

The Specific Learning Difficulties Profile and associated conditions by Jan Poustie   ISBN 1 901544 08 7

In secondary school the combination of my Dyspraxia and my Dyscalculia made my life hell as so many tasks involve motor co-ordination and number skills. My sewing was awful (the dance tunic I made fell apart the first day I wore it). Cooking was no better; the format of the recipes required that you understood ratio in order to bring the right amount of ingredients to school- and (thanks to my Dyscalculia) I didn't! PE was pretty much a nightmare, I could neither run, hit a ball or do anything well in the gym. Typing - another joy! I didn't have the muscle tone to be able to press hard enough on the keys. As for maths - don't even think about it; I existed in a mathematical fog where I could understand it one minute but the next it made no sense at all.

My whole life has been affected by my difficulties. Most of my memories are associated with things I could not do (or failed to do) rather than those in which I achieved a measure of success. I remember the Christmas present of skates (not even a chance for me to travel even the smallest distance on them thanks to my Dyspraxia), my huge distress at failing the 11+ and realising that I would not be able to join my brothers and sister at grammar school. Feeling so totally alone and alien within my secondary modern school and the sheer relief when I passed the 13+ which enabled me to attend a Grammar Technical school. Then two years of being travel sick (which often accompanies Dyspraxia) everyday on the long journey by train to the school and yet more failure. I was told that I was incapable of obtaining GSE (the old GCSE) and so would have to take the typing and shorthand course instead.

I changed schools and still my difficulties were not recognised and so I received no provision for them. The mathematics teacher commented '[she] finds this subject difficult' – an understatement if ever there was one. By now, my expressive language difficulties had reduced the 'A' for English (found in my early primary school reports) to a 50% examination grade. My inability to pass either maths or English at GCE first time meant an extra year at school. Then, having at last gained English (but failed to gain maths) I with my love of history asked if I could do 'A' level in it but was not regarded as bright enough to do so. Back to taking shorthand and typing again! Fortunately, the situation now started to change, I had a head-start in these subjects (gained through work at my previous school). Provision was now made for my muscle strength weakness through allowing me to use the only electric typewriter in the school. I succeeded so well that staff recommended that I take up teaching shorthand and typing.

Soon I was out in the big wide world as a secretary. My travel sickness had not reduced, so my daily train journey to London caused me to be sick in the Victoria Station toilets every day – and I had to pay 6p for the luxury of doing so! I then started to wonder why my boss was on his side of the desk and I was on mine! All the rest of my family were at (or were going to) university - I wanted to go too but I could not go there without maths. I found out that I had enough GCEs to gain a place at a Teacher Training College and that at just a few of these colleges one could matriculate onto a Bachelor of Education course. However, it was recommended that one had at least one 'A' level so I enrolled on an 'A' level evening class in history. After just a few lessons I realised that I could do the work easily and so without completing the course I applied to a college and talked myself into a place there. Success at last – swiftly followed by four years of hell, trying to overcome all the problems that my still unrecognised SpLD Profile conditions caused me. Despite having no 'A' levels I gained a Bachelor of Education Degree including gaining the equivalent of GCSE in Mathematics. I majored in history and drama; the latter opened my eyes to what has become the second love of my life – the theatre.

Out into the world again, but this time as a teacher. Now I found that not only did my SpLD conditions still beset me but I also had a great empathy with those who struggled to learn. And so I started to design materials and strategies to help them overcome their difficulties. I moved from the primary to the secondary sector, where I became very interested in assessment (now I also became interested in helping those with behavioural difficulties). Finally, I became Head of a Special Needs Department, although at the time I had only a small amount of knowledge on dyslexia and virtually no understanding of the other conditions that are found within the library that you are reading now.

Then my own children came along and I realised that, as is often the case, they were affected too. I felt an overwhelming desire not to let their SpLDs impact upon their lives as my difficulties had done mine. For six years I consistently worked one-hundred-hour weeks in order to find a solution for the learning difficulties of my gifted daughters. A key part of that solution was the accurate identification of their difficulties which in turn led to appropriate diagnosis and provision. Acquiring the knowledge to achieve this was not easy, the road was long, complex and hard with the situation being made worse because there was no single book or library which contained all the information that I required. During this process I fought my own SpLD conditions in order to gain two advanced teaching qualifications so that I would have the knowledge base to teach one daughter to overcome her Dyslexia and the other to overcome her Dyscalculia. At that point I had to undertake all of the provision myself as there was still a huge lack of knowledge in schools at this time.

It obvious to me that appropriate and effective provision was dependent upon accurate identification of the SpLD Profile conditions. I realised that if professionals, parents (and adults who have the conditions) are to have a chance of making a full identification of the problems faced by so many then everyone needed to have the information that I had acquired. My anguish (and my youngest daughter's distress) was so great when I struggled

Like many others who have Attention Deficits, my old school reports say it all:
- 'she must guard against inaccuracies caused by working too quickly';
- 'could apply herself more';
- 'very erratic work';
- 'must pay more attention to my instructions'.

Reading was the only thing that made my life worthwhile. It enabled me to escape from the educational reality that made my life so difficult into the world of my imagination. I gained 88% gained for reading when I was ten years old. It has continued to be the love of my life - I cannot bear to be without a book.

The Specific Learning Difficulties Profile and associated conditions by Jan Poustie   ISBN 1 901544 08 7

Many of the parents reading this library will, like me, have had a difficult educational road to travel. From the day their child starts school they fear that s/he will follow the same path as their own. The family's experiences of education may have been very bad through several generations. Grandparents may have been caned on a daily basis for the misbehaviour that the teacher knew would occur that day. Some parents may have been regularly verbally or physically humiliated in school (e.g. by being made to wear the 'dunce cap').

Such parents may fear the very professionals that they have to liaise with in order to help the child. Some may even become fearful when just entering the school building. As a result the professional may perceive them as aggressive and over-demanding. These parents will not be content with the professional observing the child for a few weeks before putting in provision, they want (and need) action and they need it now!

to gain appropriate school-based provision for her dyslexia that I had to put my thoughts to paper; this became the Gaining Provision chapter in Book 3 and from that little acorn this library has grown! Spurred on by the number of distressing stories told by professionals and parents when they rang my consultancy for help I decided to write the first edition of this library. I had no idea what I was taking on, nor the amount of my time and my life it would consume but yes, it has all been worth it. Now, thanks to my provision (and that of a specialist SpLD teacher in her final primary school) I was able last term to watch her read scientific data accessed from the internet which had a reading age well above her own age of fourteen years. Today I found out that my eldest daughter, who is beset by the same problems as myself, has passed her GCSE's (with nine A*-C grades) including mathematics!

During my research into my children's difficulties I began to recognise and identify the causes of my own educational difficulties. I have been able to accept my SpLD profile and the fact that my daughters had inherited their profiles from me without feeling guilty. Unfortunately, so many parents feel terrible guilt (and anxiety for their children's future) when they recognise their own difficulties in their children. This makes their frustration when struggling to gain provision even greater. (Teachers can also feel guilt when they realise that their lack of knowledge in the past reduced their effectiveness in helping previous students achieve their goals.) During the five years since I wrote the first edition of this library my research into specific learning difficulties has widened. This has resulted in this second edition including a good deal of information on metabolic dysfunction and the effects of diet and chemicals on the student's learning functioning. My consultancy has evolved too so that I now provide in-service training to local education authorities.

My SpLD Profile ensured that I achieved very little success in my childhood but the knowledge base and expertise that I have gained since then has helped my children (and the students with whom I work) to succeed. I wanted to design the SpLD library that was needed in the past, when I was the child, and is needed now by professionals, adults and parents. I hope that I have succeeded and that you find it of assistance both to yourself and in helping those around you. I also hope that the information found in this library makes as much difference to your life (and those whom you support) as it did to mine.

Best wishes

Jan

INTRODUCTION
The Specific Learning Difficulties Profile

PART 1 – The SpLD Profile conditions

In the past, it was believed by many that these conditions were related to each other primarily through the area of language. However, research and observation enable us to see far more links between these conditions, both with regard to their effects and their causes. We know that these conditions can affect behaviour, memory for certain types of information, and language – both mathematical, musical and the normal (native) language that we read, hear and write on an everyday basis. Thus, SpLD Profile individuals may have a combination of language-based difficulties that can be seen in any, or all, of the areas of written, spoken and heard language, plus that of body language. The appropriate use of language, together with information processing, understanding and acquiring the areas of language, can all be affected. Individuals will also have a subset of wide-ranging difficulties (for example, visual, auditory, memory, perceptual, planning, processing, behavioural and communication difficulties), each of which range from severe to low-level problems. So, we now realise that the various conditions within the Specific Learning Difficulties Profile affect literacy, numeracy, movement, behaviour, social skills and language and that we usually see more than one condition present at once.

Specific Language Impairment (also known as dysphasia)
A continuum of difficulties experienced by children and young people who have not reached expected competence in communication skills in their first language, and whose teaching and learning is consequently affected. The condition causes difficulties with expressive language (that which you speak or write) and receptive language (that which you hear or read). Often this group is defined by exclusion:

> They are not autistic, the impairment is not the result of a physical, intellectual or hearing impairment . . .(Norma Corkish, AFASIC)

Dyscalculia
Developmental Dyscalculia: Difficulties in understanding, processing and using numerical/mathematical information. It is often accompanied by one or more of the other conditions found within the Specific Learning Difficulty Profile.

Acquired Dyscalculia: As above, but caused by conditions that are not present from birth, such as ME.

The identification, assessment and management of Dyscalculia is a huge topic. So, the information on Dyscalculia that was originally in the first edition of this book has now been transferred and vastly

No two individuals will be alike and many will have more than one condition. Associated with the SpLD Profile are atopic conditions such as hayfever, eczema, asthma and nettlerash. Travel sickness can also occur and this is associated with the presence of certain aspects of Dyspraxia.

Mathematics

Various difficulties can be seen as part of Dyscalculia. Thus the student can have problems with:

▸ using or reading the correct operation sign/numeral,

▸ layout of the sum,

▸ the calculation process.

Expressive language difficulties in mathematics can cause problems in writing the sum and its various steps.

Receptive language difficulties can cause problems in reading the sum when it is set out in symbols (e.g. 3 + 2 =) and in understanding and reading word problems. It can also cause problems when the student has to translate mathematical language into his/her mother tongue so that the information can be understood.

extended to form another title. Readers interested in this topic should access *Mathematics Solutions – An Introduction to Dyscalculia: Parts A and B* by Jan Poustie (published by Next Generation).

Autistic Spectrum Disorder (used to be called Autistic Continuum): Difficulties in social interaction, social communication and imagination-based activities/behaviour.

Central Auditory Processing Disorder: A dysfunction of the processing of auditory input causing problems with understanding/ processing what is heard.

Attention Deficits (also known as Attention Deficit Disorder, Attention Deficit Hyperactivity Disorder and Behaviour Inhibition Disorder): Causes difficulties in concentrating/focusing attention and memorising information. It affects behaviour and has several forms.

Dyspraxia (also known as Developmental Dyspraxia, Developmental Coordination Disorder, sensory integration problems, coordination difficulties and motor-learning problems): There are various forms, all of which relate to difficulties in motor planning and organisation. It can affect the ability to cope with sensory stimuli and perceptual difficulties and can affect speech, eye, limb, body, hand and finger movements.

Dyslexia (also called Developmental Dyslexia): In the past, this has been used as an umbrella term for several of the conditions found within the SpLD Profile. Nowadays, it is more appropriate to use this term only in respect of a condition where the main difficulties are with the acquisition and use of spelling and/or reading skills.

The following comment made by Ginny Stacy in video entitled *A Taste of Dyslexia* applies to all of the conditions within the SpLD Profile.

> Dyslexia is not curable, but the worst of it is avoidable providing a dyslexic child is allowed to learn according to his/her natural way. This means that early recognition and appropriate teaching methods are vital; they reduce the severity of the dyslexia. Avoidance of inappropriate early learning is the nearest thing to a 'cure for dyslexia'.

One explanation of the appearance of the SpLD Profile conditions in the human species may be the increased creativity often found in individuals who have these conditions. If a person lacks the ability to organise information in any area, then s/he will have difficulties in understanding and using it unless s/he can impose his/her own form of order upon it and accept the order imposed by others. It is difficult to accept the latter unless one has the ability to see information from another person's point of view. Therefore, those who have the greatest difficulty in creating order (or accepting forms of order created by others) will have the most difficulty in gaining academic and life skills.

The Specific Learning Difficulties Profile and associated conditions by Jan Poustie   ISBN 1 901544 08 7

Imposing one's own order upon information requires original and innovative thinking. Without original thought, and the innovations associated with it, the human species could not evolve. Books have been written giving a positive image of certain conditions; e.g. *The Gift of Dyslexia* but it may be that our perception is at fault here. Perhaps those affected by the SpLD Profile conditions do not have a 'gift of a particular condition' but are themselves nature's gift to the human species without whom we could not evolve so quickly!

PART 2 – Cause or outcome?

It is becoming increasingly obvious that Dyslexia, Dyscalculia and Dyspraxia can be viewed in many students as outcomes of the presence of other Specific Learning Difficulties rather than the causal condition that lies at the root of their difficulty in learning. Alternatively, they may reflect the presence of one of the conditions frequently found alongside the Profile that are mentioned in this book.

Conceptualisation
In literacy, once a word is encoded (written or read) a conceptual leap has to be made that involves the meaning of the word in isolation and its meaning in a particular phrase, sentence or paragraph. In the language of mathematics a similar conceptual leap has to be made once the sum has been written. However, mathematics differs from literacy in that once a sum has been encoded (e.g. written down) the decoding takes place in the form of certain processes/sequences/steps whereby complex information must be retained and used in working memory. In literacy working memory has to be used for:

➤ the spelling of the word and the construction of its letters and their joins

➤ remembering both the construction of the sentence and the 'thread' of the information/story which is being written.

Memory
Working memory difficulties make it difficult (if not impossible) to retain enough information in the mind (and keep it in the right order) to complete the calculation or spelling/sentence. Auditory working memory difficulties can be identified through the use of the Digit Test (with the saying of the digits backwards informing the assessor of the extent of the problem). In the student who has Dyslexia accessing the spelling of the word can be a problem. If Specific Language Impairment is present then accessing the word itself can be difficult.

Coding and decoding
Developmental Dyslexia is now regarded by some as mainly a difficulty in coding and encoding at single-word level; for example,

Eczema and/or asthma are frequently seen alongside the SpLD Profile conditions. Adelle Davis in *Let's Get Well* (ISBN 0 7225 2701 2) provides advice on feeding formula-fed babies with a particular supplement to reduce the likelihood of one type of eczema occurring. (Her book also includes advice on other nutrients that help to take to reduce/avoid eczema and acne.)

Digit Test
This test can be found as part of different education assessment tools used by educational psychologists (e.g. WISC and BAS) and teachers (e.g. DEST, pub. The Psychological Corporation, Tel: 02083 085700 and the Aston Index, pub. LDA, Tel: 01945 63441).

the building up and breaking down of words into their smallest parts, called phonemes or sound patterns. This involves the processing and understanding of simple concepts via abstract symbols; for example, letters. In spelling the position of symbols is everything; for example, 'fish' is correct but 'fihs' is not. However, in the spelling of mathematics position is relevant only at certain times; for example, 10 + 2 is the same as 2 + 10 but 10 − 2 and 2 − 10 do not have similar outcomes. In the number 123 the '2' has the value of twenty whilst in 213 it has the value of two hundred. Here, the order (sequence) of the numerals matters.

Planning, prioritising and organising information

Decision making can be a major problem for those who have any of the conditions within the SpLD Profile. Those who have Developmental Dyspraxia find many planning and organisational tasks particularly difficult (see *Planning and Organisation Solutions* , ISBN 1 901544 81 8 and *Creative and Factual Writing Solutions*, ISBN 1 901544 38 9, both by Jan Poustie, for further information).

Those who have Autistic Spectrum Disorder (ASD) and/or Attention Deficits (ADD/ADHD), fail to categorise and prioritise information in a way that is acceptable to other individuals. ASD individuals are also frequently unable to accept the categorisation and prioritisation of information produced by others, this may also occur with those who have ADD/ADHD. This problem is in itself both an outcome and a cause of difficulties. Classification is not a simple skill, as the following example shows when we try to define the word 'woman'. 'Woman' is an interpretation of various factors (e.g. the presence of long hair and breasts) which has to be defined further if information is presented in a slightly different format (e.g. a woman can have short hair and small breasts). Overweight men can have breasts and all men have some degree of breast tissue. Therefore, we have to further define the word by looking at internal attributes rather than the superficial ones (e.g. uterus). However, a woman remains a woman despite a hysterectomy which removes the womb!!! So, to be absolutely sure that we know just what a 'woman' is we have to go to the genetic level (e.g. a woman has two X chromosomes and men have an X and a Y chromosome).

Sequencing

When severe Dyslexia is present, the person cannot accurately remember a sequence or match symbol to sound. When Dyscalculia is present the difficulty is in matching a symbol (numeral) to its value and remembering the sequence of the spelling (writing) of the sum and the process by which the sum is worked out. The person who has Dyspraxia will have difficulties in remembering the sequence of movements needed to achieve a given action; e. g. do up a zip or write a word using cursive (joined-up) writing.

Making the task suit the student's interests makes an emotional link to the work and so teaching becomes more effective.

The foundation level of literacy and numeracy

The foundation level of learning in each discipline is slightly different. In numeracy Professor Mahesh Sharma has identified nine areas at the concrete operational stage of learning that must be complete in order for numeracy acquisition to progress normally. In the case of literacy, we know that phonological skills must be present. In both areas, the individual must be able to write symbols, know the meaning/value of the symbol, and be able to write each symbol in a particular order defined by set rules.

Developmental Dyscalculia can be regarded as difficulties in the coding of simple concepts via the abstract symbols found in sums; e. g. 1 + 2=. To encode a word, you have to know which of the symbols go where and this placement is defined by rules such as those found in spelling (e.g. long 'a' sound, as in ape, is written 'ake' in the word 'lake' but short 'a' sound as in 'apple' is written 'ack', as in 'lack'). In encoding sums, you have to know where the parts of the sum go when writing a sum or a pair of digits; e.g. 6 ÷ 2 or 2 ÷ 6.

Processing of information

In both literacy and numeracy, language is important for both the understanding of concepts and the recording of information. In both areas, the student has to be able to accurately process what s/he hears so that explanations of concepts, spellings etc. (and the linking of them to particular symbols) are understood. Finally, the student has to process what s/he sees in a particular way so that there are no distortions of the symbols viewed. It is these latter two areas that are most important since students who cannot accurately process what their senses tell them cannot even enter the learning arena.

It is important to realise that the SpLD Profile conditions do not just affect a student's learning. They also may affect many (if not all areas) of his/her life. Language difficulties may make it difficult for the student to achieve and maintain long-term relationships. Motor coordination difficulties make it difficult to do the many practical tasks involved in running a home. Communication and auditory processing difficulties may make it difficult to use a telephone. Literacy difficulties may make travel stressful, as there are so many signs in railway stations, on the roads and so on. Numeracy difficulties cause problems when doing DIY tasks, cooking and when travelling. For more details, see *Life Skills* by Jan Poustie, ISBN 1 901544 50 8.

The most effective way of reducing these problems is to give the individual appropriate and effective provision as early as possible. However, such provision can only be achieved once the cause of the problem is known, hence the need for early identification and the reason why this library was written. However, identification of the conditions is only the first step, In order to meet the needs of the

Information processing
We can expect visual perceptual difficulties to interfere with learning when Dyspraxia is present, whilst auditory processing difficulties can be seen as part of Central Auditory Processing Disorder. Research has now been conducted which indicates that there is a link between Dyslexia and a difference in the performance of the visual pathways of the brain. (For further information see Book 4 of this library.)

The Specific Learning Difficulties Profile and associated conditions by Jan Poustie   ISBN 1 901544 08 7

student, parent and teacher (and reduce alienation between all three parties) we need to find out their views on the areas of difficulty and what they want provision to focus upon. Ways in which to find out these (often different) views can be found in Appendix 4 of this book.

CHAPTER 1
Conditions found alongside the SpLD Profile

Meares-Irlen Syndrome
(also known as Scotopic Sensitivity Irlen Syndrome). *This section is by Patricia Clayton (Irlen diagnostician) and edited by Jan Poustie.*

Meares-Irlen Syndrome is a perceptual dysfunction affecting reading- and writing-based activities, as well as depth perception. Individuals need to put more energy and effort into the reading process because they are inefficient readers, seeing the page differently from 'good' readers. Constant adaptation to distortions from print or the white background causes fatigue and discomfort and, more importantly, limits the length of time these individuals can read and maintain comprehension. If the syndrome is undetected, affected people, although often appearing bright, may be viewed as underachievers with poor behavioural attitudes or motivational problems, and/or incorrectly labelled as being of low ability. It is a perceptual dysfunction caused by sensitivity to light rather than a visual problem of a refractive nature. This syndrome causes reading to deteriorate and become slow and hesitant. Any of the following may be present:

▸ poor reading comprehension,

▸ inability to sustain reading for any length of time (difficult to spot using conventional reading tests as students may do well for ten minutes and then begin to fade),

▸ skipping of words/lines, misreading of words,

▸ slow reading rate,

▸ avoids reading,

▸ trouble in tracking,

▸ background seen as too bright (glare), print as indistinct, a need to read in dim lighting.

Meares-Irlen Syndrome can aggravate other learning disorders and physical disabilities, which may be shown in the following ways:

▸ *Physical:* individuals are clumsy and uncoordinated, have difficulty in catching balls, drive extremely cautiously, cannot judge distances, are unable to sit still, suffer from motion sickness.

▸ *Writing:* individuals write up or downhill, exhibit unequal spacing, and make errors when copying.

▸ *Reading:* individuals need to put more effort and energy into the reading process.

▸ *Maths:* individuals are criticised for sloppy/careless maths

Meares-Irlen Syndrome

Neurological research suggests that the Irlen filter technique allows receptor cells in the visual cortex to analyse visual information more efficiently by selectively filtering the input of specific wavelengths of light. The Irlen filters are specially modified filters in a very wide range of different colour combinations. They will reduce eye-strain, headaches and migraine in individuals affected by Meares-Irlen Syndrome.

Assessment is by consultation with a specialist at an Irlen Centre (see end of book) who will carry out an intensive diagnostic interview to determine which combination of the different Irlen filters will be most beneficial. Individuals with problems that cannot be rectified by the use of filters will be referred to other specialists. (Also see Book 3 of the library.)

Recommended reading for visual difficulties

▸   Chapter 7: 'Vision problems - their effects on learning, and how to help, both at home and in the classroom', *Literacy Solutions* by Jan Poustie, pub. Next Generation.

▸   Book 4 of the library: *Identification Solutions for Literacy* which looks at Dyslexia and Near-vision Dysfunctioning.

errors, misalignment of numbers.

▸   *Music:* individuals have difficulty in reading music and play better by ear.

▸   *General:* individuals exhibit general strain or fatigue, falling asleep, headaches or nausea, watery eyes, eye strain, hot/ dry eyes, low self-esteem, withdrawn behaviour, sensitivity to noise, faulty perception of colour, difficulties in looking at a computer screen.

▸   *Academic:* individuals display an inability to concentrate, start work, and organise thoughts. They search for words, have difficulty in expressing ideas clearly, are hesitant and use jumbled expressions when explaining ideas. They divert attention to avoid completing tasks and need frequent repetition of instructions.

Recommended reading

📖   *Reading by the Colours* by Helen Irlen (ISBN 0 89529 482 6, Published by Avery Publishing Group). Explains the condition and how it can be helped through the use of Irlen lenses.

Genetically Inherited Syndromes
A wide variety of genetically inherited syndromes exist, of which several can include specific learning difficulties as part of their characteristics. Each student affected by a genetically inherited syndrome will have a different set of difficulties, so the literacy strategies will vary according to the areas of greatest difficulty. Attention will also need to be paid to any relevant research into effective learning strategies with regard to the particular syndrome affecting the student. If you need to know more about an unusual condition then look in *The CaF Directory – Index of Specific Conditions and Rare Disorders* which can be found at http://www.cafamily.org.uk/home.html

Fragile X
Many individuals show features commonly associated with autism; e.g. a dislike of eye contact, difficulty in relating to other people, anxiety in social situations often leading to tantrums, insistence on familiar routines and hand flapping or hand biting. Speech and language is usually delayed with continuing speech difficulties and some children and adults develop epilepsy.

Fragile X Syndrome
Second only to Downs Syndrome as the most common cause of learning disability, Fragile X Syndrome is the most common inherited cause of learning disability. It occurs more in boys than girls and is associated with varying degrees of learning difficulty. Boys affected by the condition almost always have some learning difficulty, ranging from mild to severe learning difficulties (it accounts 'for almost 10% of all boys with moderate to profound learning disabilities'[1]). Girls are often of normal intelligence but up to a third have learning problems that which may be mild, moderate, or occasionally severe. Frequent episodes of glue ear, can occur (this is thought to be a 'substantial problem for 60%'[2] of those who have Fragile X[3]). Behaviours include short attention span, distractibility, impulsiveness and overactivity.[4] Shyness and social withdrawal are often seen in girls, and may create difficulties in making friends.

Identifying: Fragile X Syndrome should be suspected in any person having some combination of the following characteristics:

➥ unexplained developmental delay (irrespective of the degree of severity)

➥ a likeable, happy, friendly personality combined with a limited number of the social difficulties commonly associated with autism (see Book 6)

➥ unusual and repetitive patterns of speech

➥ hyperactivity and poor impulse control.

Referral: It is recommended that any individual exhibiting unexplained developmental delay (irrespective of degree of severity) or autism of unknown cause should be tested for Fragile X. Diagnosis is established by a Fragile X DNA test, usually on a blood sample. This can be arranged by a GP, paediatrician or clinical geneticist.

For further information on this condition contact The Fragile X Society (see their details at the end of this book).

Notes and References

1. & 2. Graham, P., Turk J., and Verhulst F., (1999) *Child Psychiatry: A developmental Approach*, Oxford University Press.

3. Note that glue ear is also associated with CAPD (see Book 3 of the library).

4. Such behaviours are also associated with Attention Deficits (see Book 6 of the library).

Metabolic functioning

Thyroid conditions

The metabolic system is controlled by various glands, of which the thyroid gland is of prime importance to our emotional balance. Problems can arise if it becomes overactive (hyperthyroidism) or underactive (hypothyroidism) which then causes various difficulties including behaviours commonly associated with ADHD. Emotional, physical or mental stress (e.g. from examinations, slimming, family break-up) and a variety of foods can affect thyroid function. Women can find it very difficult to keep their weight down when hypothyroidism is present. A great deal of research has been conducted into thyroid problems which has resulted in 'the discovery that an imbalance of thyroid hormone in the brain can be responsible for Attention Deficit Hyperactivity Disorder' [when a] 'Syndrome of thyroid hormone resistance' is present.[1] 'In these patients, a genetic defect causes the thyroid hormone to work less efficiently in the brain, pituitary, and other organs'[2] Thyroid problems can affect both children and adults.

Non-verbal Learning Deficit (NLD)
'This is associated with a deficiency of white matter in the brain. Such individuals have marked difficulties in the processing of visuospatial information which will affect symbolic language, geometry, writing/layout, map reading, reading diagrams and the use of planning and organisational tools.' (Martin Turner, Head of Psychology, Dyslexia Institute).

This term is being used in some quarters to include forms of Dyspraxia and Childhood Hemiplegia. Bryon Rourke is a neuropsychologist based in Canada. Further information on NLD, including Bryon Rourke's answers to commonly asked questions on NLD, can be found at the following internet site: www. nldontheweb.org/little_1.htm

📖 **Recommended Reading**
Syndrome of Non-Verbal Learning Disabilities by Byron Rourke (ISBN 0898623782, published by Guilford Publications).

Hypothyroidism
(The juvenile form commonly occurs at eight years though it can occur as young as five years and may be accompanied by a slowdown in growth.[3])
Usually a gradual onset/steady deterioration in function occurs with any of the following being seen:

Physical effects: slight swelling in the neck, mildly overweight for height, small appetite, clumsy.

Mental effects: memory, concentration and language difficulties. The person appears 'increasingly slow (mentally and physically), clumsy, inattentive and apparently lazy'[4]

Hyperthyroidism
(In childhood, onset is usually at about ten years though it can occur as young as five. It may be accompanied by bedwetting and frequent bowel movements.)
The individual has a predisposition to the illness which is set off by a stressor; e.g. an illness, emotional stress or such like. Any of the following can be seen: difficulties in all relationships; concentration difficulties; fidgeting; moody, uncooperative or rebellious behaviour; a large appetite; and rapid fatigue.

Referral
Is via one's GP for thyroid tests (using a blood sample). Each form requires different medication which will take time to reduce the symptoms. Some people with thyroid dysfunction find that even with medication they never return to a feeling of being totally well. Note that iron interferes with the absorption of thyroid hormones so if thyroid deficiency is present do not take iron along with your thyroxine. (See *The Thyroid Solution* by Dr Ridha Arem, page 248.)

Recommended Reading
- *Coping with Thyroid Problems* by Dr Joan Gomez ISBN 085969 687 1 (pub. Sheldon Press) contains an excellent section on childhood forms of thyroid disorder.
- *Thyroid Problems: a Practical Guide to Symptoms and Treatment* by Patsy Westcott ISBN 07225 31648 (pub. Thorsons Health) As many more women than men develop thyroid disease this book, which is devoted to women, is exceptionally useful.
- *The Thyroid Solution* by Dr. Ridha Arem ISBN 0345 42920 6 (pub. Ballantine) This excellent book, written by an American doctor, provides information on how taking a combination of thyroid hormones can improve mental functioning.

Essential fatty acids (EFAs) and Trace Elements
The research into this comparatively new area to the field of Specific Learning Difficulties focuses (at present) on the Omega-3 (n-3) and Omega-6 (n-6) essential fatty acids. It is now apparent that some of our students need to take supplements of these oils to improve their functioning (both academic and behavioural). However, the question of who is likely to benefit from them and which oils should be taken

References and Notes
1. Arem, R., *The Thyroid Solution*, ISBN 0345 42920 6, published by Ballantine.
2. P. Hauser, A. J. Zametkin, P. Martinex, et al., 'Attention Deficit-Hyperactivity Disorder in People with Generalized Resistance to Thyroid Hormone,' *New England Journal of Medicine* 328 no. 14 (1993): 997-1001, cited in *The Thyroid Solution* by Dr. Ridha Arem ISBN 0345 42920 6, published Ballantine.
3. Arem, R., *The Thyroid Solution*, ISBN 0345 42920 6, published Ballantine.
4. Less common is early childhood hypothyroidism, the effects of which are seen during baby/toddlerhood; see *Coping with Thyroid Problems* by Dr Joan Gomez ISBN 085969 687 1 for details.

(via supplements or EFA rich foods) has now become the focus of interest for many people.

> The bottom line here is that EFAs are required for normal functioning of every cell, tissue, gland and organ. Most people get too little n-3. N-3 intake in the population is down to 1/6th of what people obtained in diets in 1850. N-6 intake has doubled over the past 100 years, mostly by emphasis on corn and safflower oils, which are rich in n-6 and contain almost no n-3. People on low fat diets get too little of both n-3 and n-6. If the body obtains enough of both of these in their basic form (as alpha-linolenic acid (LNA) and linoleic acid (LA)) and in the right ratio of LNA to LA, the body converts these to long chain derivatives. It needs both the basic EFAs and the long chain derivatives.
> Dr Udo Erasmus, *Nutritionist*

Consumption of fats

The twentieth century saw a vast change in our diet (more sweets and starches) and a great decrease in the amount of physical exercise most of us undertake. The result was a huge increase in obesity. This in turn led to people adopting low-fat diets, because, in the words of Dr Udo Erasmus, 'most people erroneously think that eating fats is the reason for getting fat, which is not true', with a consequent loss of energy levels and/or compromised immune function in some people. Others have found that they have developed leaky gut syndrome leading to food intolerance and/or allergies, which can appear as Irritable Bowel Syndrome. The diet of too many individuals now bears little relationship to the more natural and thus more healthy diet found during the middle of the twentieth century. A look into the supermarket trolley reveals that, in many cases, we have moved away from hard fats (e.g. butter) to the trans-fatty acids. The trans-fatty acids (e.g. hydrogenated or partially hydrogenated oils found in margarine, shortening and convenience foods) do not normally occur in nature but are found in many processed foods (including hydrogenated peanut butter, the staple food of so many children!). Various researchers working across the world have found out a great deal about fats in general (including EFAs) and trans-fatty acids in particular. Trans-fatty acids have been found to change the way our fat cells and immune system works, and also change the cell membranes within our body. They also interfere with the functioning of the essential fatty acids within our body and, according to Dr Udo Erasmus, are associated with increased cancer, cardiovascular disease, liver detoxification problems, visual problems in children, lower IQ, slower learning and poorer reproduction (in animals).

Oils versus hard fats

Except for virgin or unrefined oils (such as cold pressed green olive oil and oils made with health rather than shelf life in mind) oil is

What are the essential fatty acids?

Omega-3 (alpha-linolenic acid) and Omega-6 (linoleic acid) are the two that we are most concerned with. They are sensitive to destruction by light, oxygen and high temperature (and become toxic when we fry them!). They increase energy production in the body by helping it to obtain more oxygen.

Those who are diabetic and are taking supplements rich in Omega 3 should have their requirements for insulin regularly monitored as this EFA decreases the need for injected insulin.

The Specific Learning Difficulties Profile and associated conditions by Jan Poustie   ISBN 1 901544 08 7

The fact that in Canada the law prohibits the use of trans-fatty acids in baby food should be giving us all 'food for thought'.

Deprive a rat of Omega-3 and the mother will produce pups that have permanent learning disabilities. It is believed that the brain will take what it needs from the resources available and that in brain tissue the proportion of Omega-3 to Omega-6 is 1:1. Both of these EFAs are found in breast milk.

Is the diet of our pregnant mothers affecting the amount of the EFAs in the foetal brain and could this (and the fact that in the past, few formula milks contained Omega-3) be two of the reasons for the increase in the number of children with learning and behavioural difficulties? The short answer is YES.

processed by being degummed (treated with chemicals such as those used to clean kitchen drains) and refined using an extremely corrosive acid. Then it is bleached, which leaves an unpleasant smell and taste that is reduced by deodorising. During this process, the oil is heated to above frying temperature, some beneficial ('minor') ingredients are removed, some of the EFAs are destroyed and toxic molecules are formed. If we use oils which have a good reputation (e.g. those richest in EFAs such as flax, sunflower or olive oil) in cooking processes involving high heat; e.g. for frying, they are the ones which become most toxic. Eating too many hard fats (e.g. hard cheese, fatty meat) instead of EFA-rich oils will interfere with insulin production (see page 11) and affect the functioning of EFAs. Hard fats produce energy but in our modern society we generally perform less labour intensive tasks than our forebears and so we need a lot less of this type of fat in our diet, especially as the more hard fat we eat the more EFAs we need to eat!

The relationship between sugars and fats

Just to make our lives a little more difficult, we then come to the issue of sugar. Yes, we know it is not a fat, but too much sugar in the diet moves insulin function toward diabetes and interferes with the functioning of essential fatty acids. It can also increase adrenalin production (by up to 400%) – is this part of the reason why we are seeing so many more behavioural problems in our schools? Sugar is also converted by the body into the wrong kind of fat. Sugar cannot be converted into the essential fats. Unfortunately, it does not matter which type of sugar we eat (e.g. honey, syrup and so on) they all have the same effect on the body.

There is a growing body of evidence indicating the undesirability of reducing the sugars in our diet by replacing them with artificial sweeteners; e.g. in soft drinks. Some professionals believe that aspects of the brain functioning, (e.g. headaches and memory), vision and behaviour, (e.g. mood swings), can be affected and there are concerns that children (both in the womb and in childhood) are especially vulnerable. The evidence on aspartame given to the UK's Food Advisory Committee (published in a discussion paper dated 26th October 2000, Agenda Item 7) raises concerns regarding the effects of this sweetener especially with regard to children. Current EU/UK laws do not permit aspartame or any other sweetener in products for children under 36 months; e.g. weaning foods. However, there does not appear to be a regulation requiring that warnings appear on products containing aspartame which might be given to young children such as sweets and soft drinks. The two major concerns regarding aspartame have been linked with the presence of phenylalanine and methanol. Some professionals fear that the increased levels of phenylalanine could result in an imbalance which could then affect the developing brain of the child. Methanol (methyl alcohol) is produced when aspartame is broken down.

Who benefits from essential fatty acid supplements?

Every man, woman and child requires EFAs for health. A list of indicators of Omega-3 and Omega-6 deficiencies can be found at the www.equazen.com website. We appear to have three groups of students that might benefit from essential fatty acid supplements:

1. Those born with a metabolic dysfunction which results in them not being able to process essential fatty acids properly.

2. Those who need a larger amount of EFAs in their diet because their diet is affecting the functioning of the EFAs that they do eat.

3. Those with fungal infections; e.g. candida (thrush) and athlete's foot.

Achieving the correct ratio of EFAs in our diet

Too much of one of these oils will result in a deficiency in the other as each of them competes for enzyme space in our cells. Thus, flax oil is too rich in Omega-3 for long-term use. Based upon two forms of healthy diet we can see what the upper limits of this balance are likely to be; e.g. the Inuit (Eskimo) diet has the highest ratio: 2.5:1 (e.g. one tablespoon of Omega-3 for every teaspoon of Omega-6). The Mediterranean diet has a ratio of 1:6 (one teaspoon of Omega-3 for every six teaspoons of Omega-6).

Factors to be taken into consideration with regard to EFAs

Do not take a high concentration of EFAs too close to bedtime because they can boost one's energy and so cause difficulties in sleeping. High doses of EFAs may also cause nausea. Occasionally some people have an allergic response to EFA oils. Dr Udo Erasmus in *Fats that Heal, Fats that Kill* recommends spreading intake of oil (usually between 15ml per 50 pounds and 15ml per 100 pounds of body weight per day) over the course of the day, mixed in foods, so as not to overload the liver's capacity for processing oils. Taking digestive enzymes may help the body to process the EFA oils. Various factors affect the body's ability to convert EFAs into Highly Unsaturated Fatty Acids (HUFAs); e.g. excess caffeine, alcohol, smoking and stress. Caffeine is found in chocolate, coffee, tea, some cold remedies, cola and energy drinks.

> Low dietary and body levels of the minerals magnesium and zinc, and the vitamins B3, B6 and C can slow down the conversion of EFAs into long chain derivatives. Insufficient intake of EFAs also (obviously) makes it impossible to convert enough into long chain derivatives.
>
> Dr Udo Erasmus, *Nutritionist.*

Aspartame (E951)

> 10% of the aspartame taken into the body turns into methyl alcohol. Methyl alcohol can damage vision and brain functioning

Dr Udo Erasmus, *Nutritionist*

There appears to be a great deal of debate about aspartame with various research reports coming to different conclusions. To see both sides of this issue:

➤ Type all of the following words into your internet search engine: aspartame, methyl, alcohol.

➤ Go to the UK government site to see the discussion paper mentioned on page 12: www.foodstandards.gov.uk/ pdf_files/papers/ fac_sweet_45.pdf

Warning: remember when taking supplements and foods rich in Omega 3 that they will also contain Vitamin A. An excess of Vitamin A can be harmful., so avoid taking high doses of fish liver oils in particular on a regular basis.

Constitutional factors that affect EFA conversion into HUFAs include: ageing, allergies (including asthma and atopic eczema), psoriasis, and diabetes. [1] It should also be noted that males are more vulnerable to EFA deficiency than women as the oestrogen in females helps to protect them from such deficiency. [2] The following can be seen when EFA deficiency is present:

- Frequent urination and thirst.
- Dry hair and skin. Dandruff can be present.
- Visual perception problems.
- High distractibility.
- Tendency to allergies; e.g. asthma, eczema.
- Difficulties in going to sleep.
- Arthritis-like conditions.
- Dry skin, areas of skin (especially upper arms and thighs) may have a roughened/dry bumpy appearance.**
- Visual functioning can be affected; e.g. eye strain/glare.*
- Motor coordination impairment.*
- Behavioural changes.**
- Low metabolic rate.*
- Deterioration in mental ability.*

*Those items marked with an asterisk * are commonly found when an Omega-3 deficiency is present. Those marked with ** can indicate a deficiency in either Omega-3 or 6.*

Trace elements and EFAs
Zinc is a co-factor that helps build the bodies supply of HUFAs from EFAs. Researchers believe that the reason why a group of ADHD children have been found to be low in zinc may be due to changes in their gut permeability resulting in a more Leaky Gut than normal. [3] There may also be a 'knock-on effect' in that lower zinc levels affect gut permeability. Zinc deficiency has been linked to gastro intestinal changes in the enterocytes part of the gut lining and damage to the micro villi (the finger-like projections along the lining of the intestine). [4] As seminal plasma (the fluid component of semen) contains some of the highest zinc levels of any body fluid, every ejaculation removes zinc from the body. Therefore, ADHD teenage boys in particular may be at greatest risk of zinc deficiency. [5] Urinary toxic trace-element levels are also very important; e.g. cadmium has a tendency to accumulate in the kidneys and is a known antagonist to (that is, acts to stop) zinc absorption. [6] Other heavy metals (e.g. lead) and aluminium may also be found in excess in ADHD children.

Regular tests for anaemia are advisable when taking zinc. Although some people can take zinc supplements on a daily basis, others need rests from taking it if they are not to become anaemic. Vitamin C

Recommended daily zinc intake for adults is 15mg. Intake up to 60mg per day for adults is safe. Above 110mg per day, zinc can inhibit immune function
    Dr Udo Erasmus, *Nutritionist*

aids the absorption of many essential trace elements such as iron.[7] Many young children have very low levels of iron, which may be due to poor dietary intake (e.g. lack of green vegetables), inadequate body metabolism or the presence of another trace metal making it difficult to absorb and/or utilise iron (e.g. raised levels of copper).

<u>Epilepsy and essential fatty acids</u>
There is some concern that those with a predisposition towards epilepsy may be more at risk if they take EFAs.

> Our experience with epilepsy suggests that n-6 [Omega-6] may enhance susceptibility to seizures and that n-3 [Omega-3] may help to decrease susceptibility. We also find that digestive enzymes rich in protease can decrease susceptibility. Epilepsy, both in animals and humans, shows a strong correlation with poor digestion and food allergies. Enzymes work at the digestion level to nip the cause in the bud.
> Dr Udo Erasmus, *Nutritionist*

> There is some evidence that some fatty acids (notably Omega-6 fatty acids) may enhance the risk of epilepsy. In contrast other fatty acids are strongly anti-epileptic (e.g. EPA which is part of the Omega-3 series and found in fish oils) . There has been reported to be a very small risk of inducing a particular type of epilepsy known as temporal lobe epilepsy in people taking evening primrose oil. However, this is exceptionally rare and other forms of epilepsy seem to benefit from evening primrose oil.
> Dr David Horrobin, *Research Scientist*

> The real issue seems to be that the Omega-3 fatty acids clearly have a protective effect against epileptic-type activity. The balance of Omega-3 and Omega-6 is an important issue that is often overlooked and most people are more at risk for Omega-3 deficiency. It is therefore possible that supplementing with Omega-6 when the real problem is an existing Omega-3 deficiency may trip that balance further towards Omega-3 deficiency. This, rather than Omega-6 itself may be behind some of the anecdotal reports surrounding Omega-6 fatty acids and epilepsy.
> Dr Alexandra Richardson, *Senior Research Fellow in Neuroscience*

Questions we should ask when looking at EFAs
EFAs provide stable, sustained and extended energy by helping the body to obtain more oxygen. They increase energy levels, stamina and metabolic rate; enable people to recover more quickly from fatigue; and improve brain function. Some of the questions that we need to ask ourselves are reproduced below along with answers given by Dr Udo Erasmus:

Q/ Is a shortage of EFAs in the diet the reason why one reception class teacher has noticed that she has more stamina than her pupils when doing PE? Will these oils help those who have ME (Chronic/ Post-Viral Fatigue Syndrome)?

Zinc deficiency
When a zinc deficiency is present we may see:
» loss of appetite;
» failure to grow;
» skin changes (e.g. rashes, eczema etc.);
» wounds take longer to heal;
» decreased taste acuity;
» behavioural disturbances;
» increased susceptibility to infection (because of reduced immunity);
» infertility;
» birth defects (e.g. low birth weight, still birth).

Tests for zinc deficiency are;
1. An alkaline phosphatase enzyme test (via your GP).
2. A sweat test (via Biolab Medical Unit, Tel: 02076365959) plus there are many commercial laboratories that do a scalp hair test for the different trace elements).
Neil Ward, *Senior lecturer in analytical and environmental chemistry, University of Surrey, UK*

A/ At 15ml per 50 pounds of body weight they [EFAs] usually improve energy levels substantially not only in Fatigue Syndrome, but also in athletes, in those too tired to exercise, in people needing to work late on projects to meet deadlines (e.g. working all night) and in athletes pushing the limits of their performance. In a study carried out in Denmark, stamina increased by 40 to 60% in athletes on 15ml per 50 pounds of body weight within one month of beginning this regime (no other changes in diet).

Q/ Is the low-fat diet of some of our body-conscious teenage girls affecting their learning capability?

A/ Absolutely. Dry skin and low energy are usually the first signs. Eventually their liver and kidneys deteriorate. Glands dry up. Insulin does not work in the absence of EFAs. Heart beat abnormalities, increased susceptibility to infections and cancer, poor wound healing, and stunted growth in children are other symptoms of low fat diets. Cessation of the period in females and premenstrual syndrome are also associated with EFA deficiency.

Q/ Do we need to enrich the basic prison diet with EFAs in order to improve the behaviour and academic functioning of the inmates?

A/ Research indicates that EFAs make violent criminals calmer and less violent.

Q/ Is the highly processed American diet, with its effect on EFA functioning, partially responsible for the increased incidence of Attention Deficits in the USA and the UK?

A/ Research shows that children with attention deficit/hyperactivity disorder respond well to EFA enrichment of their diet.

References and Footnotes
1.&2. Alex Richardson PATOSS Conference 2001. Also see her article on Essential Fatty Acids in the PATOSS 2001 Bulletin, Vol. 14, No. 1, May 2001 (e-mail patoss@evesham.ac.uk for details).
3. Ward, N. I., 1997, 'Assessment of chemical factors in relation to child hyperactivity', *Journal of Nutritional Environmental Medicine* Vol. 7, pp 333 –42.
4. Halas, E. S., 1983, 'Behavioural Changes accompanying zinc deficiency in animals', in Dreosti, I. and Smith, R. [eds] *Neurobiology of the trace elements* Humana Press Publishers, New Jersey, pp. 213 – 43.
5. Ward, N. I., 2000, 'Chemical substances and human behaviour', *The Nutrition Practioner*, Vol. 2, pp. 43 – 5).
6. Prasad, A. S. and Oberleas, D., 1976, *Trace elements in human health and disease, Vol. 1: Zinc and copper*, published by Academic Press, New York.
7. Davis, A., 1996, *Let's Get Well*, published by George Allen & Unwin.

CHAPTER 2
Conditions causing an acquired form of the SpLD Profile

All of the conditions found within the previous chapter occur as a result of differences in the development of a child within the womb. Some conditions however, are not developmental in origin; they occur either after the individual is born (as in ME) or just before birth/in the first few years of life as a result of an insult (injury) to the brain (e.g. Childhood Hemiplegia). The individual is said to have an acquired form of the SpLD Profile. Some children have major problems in learning because they have both a developmental and an acquired form of the SpLD Profile, as the case study of Bethany shows (see page 21).

Childhood Hemiplegia
This is caused by brain damage as a result of haemorrhages in the brain just before birth, at birth or in the first few years of life. (Two-thirds will be of normal intelligence, the other third are likely to be of less than normal intelligence.) Most of the children who have moderate to severe damage are likely to be affected by specific learning difficulties. Those with mild damage are less likely to be affected by SpLD. There can be difficulties in reading, spelling and arithmetic. Non-verbal skills are the most likely to be affected, with language skills being preserved whilst visuospatial skills are lost to some extent; i.e. similar difficulties to those found in Non-verbal Learning Deficit. Movement, behavioural, emotional and social skills difficulties may also be present. Assessment of the student's cognitive functioning is by a paediatric neuropsychologist, of which there is a shortage in the UK. Referral to such a professional is via the child's GP, who can locate the nearest one. There are specialist neuropsychological centres at Great Ormond Street Hospital (London) and at The Radcliffe Hospital, Oxford.

Myalgic Encephalomyelitis (ME)
ME is also known Post-Viral Fatigue Syndrome (PVFS), Chronic Fatigue and Immune Dysfunction Syndrome (CFIDS) and Chronic Fatigue Syndrome (CFS), with some professionals believing it is a sub-group of the latter condition. In the past PVFS has been used for short-term 'fatigue-based' illnesses that occur after viral infections. The terms ME or CFS tend to have been used when the condition is long term. In Britain, the favoured term now for all of these is Chronic Fatigue Syndrome/ME (abbreviated to CFS/ME). For convenience, the term ME is used in this book.

Childhood Hemiplegia
It appears that an insult to the brain (haemorrhage) may not always result in the loss of movement of one side of the body. Some children appear to have their physical functioning intact but their cognitive (intellectual) functioning and behaviour affected. This non-hemiplegic group may have similar academic difficulties as those affected by childhood hemiplegia.

'There are around 25,000 young people in the UK who have ME.' (Action for ME Young People Update).

There is a better chance of recovery if the student receives enough rest during the initial stages of ME. (This initial stage may take weeks, months or years.)

Temperature control may fluctuate; for example, hands and feet (or the whole body) may be very cold one minute and too hot the next. Those suffering from ME may need to be snuggled up on the sofa under a duvet with the central heating full on.

A GP will either diagnose ME or will refer the child to a paediatrician for diagnosis. It is usually a long-term illness, characterised by fatigue, muscle pain and flu-like symptoms, which occur after little or no mental/physical effort, and which can last for several years. Both children (from as young as five years) and adults are affected by the condition (there is some evidence that females are more likely to contract the illness than males). The recovery process takes about two and a half years but it should be noted that few return to 100% fitness. ME recovery figures for all groups of children show that 25% return to near normal functioning, 25% to less than a quarter of their original functioning and 50% to approximately half of their original functioning. Research has shown that children who contract the illness during the autumn term (and those who had a sudden onset of the condition) tend to recover faster. For those for whom the condition developed slowly the future may be more bleak. (See *M.E. Post-Viral Fatigue Syndrome: how to live with it* by Dr Anne Macintyre.)

ME causes changes in the brain chemistry that result in the person developing an acquired form of the SpLD Profile, which will disappear or reduce as the student recovers from the illness. The student can be too tired to look at print or work out a simple sum. We may see problems in many areas; e.g. mathematics (especially in the area of arithmetic), spelling and language skills – both expressive and receptive – may deteriorate, and physical skills and balance are also likely to be affected. Feeding oneself may be so fatiguing that the sufferer will only be able to eat a little food at each meal. It may take too much energy to maintain a good posture and so the student slumps in the seat, or finds it more comfortable and less fatiguing to lie down. Problems with muscle fatigue (and with controlling the movements of the eye and also with glare) cause the student to have difficulty reading and watching television.

The very nature of ME makes it difficult for students and adults around them to understand/cope with the condition. One minute the student may appear to be hyperactive; the next s/he may be listless and unable to concentrate. Concentration, language skills and memory can be badly affected. The student may be unable to retain new information, and may forget events that happen during the day and/or that happened in earlier years. All of this can cause the student considerable distress. When the condition is at its worst, the student may be extremely sensitive to light and/or sound and so may have to lie in a quiet, dark room. (Many students will find throughout the illness that they cannot tolerate people raising their voices around them and so are easily stressed.) Students often find it difficult to maintain their social links, as they soon may have little in common with their friends, having very little energy for social activities outside of school.

Recovery is only likely to occur if the student has enough bed rest at the start of the illness. (All too often, schools and LEAs expect these children to return to school too quickly and for too many lessons.) Once an improvement is seen, they need tuition provided by an LEA home tutor (up to five hours per week is the usual amount). Once they can cope easily with this amount of tuition, they need a mixed provision whereby they receive some LEA home tuition plus some time in school. In some cases it can take several years to reach this level of functioning. Some students will stay at this level for several years before being able to progress to an increased number of lessons. Some will be able gradually to increase their time at school and eventually may be able to return to full-time schooling, though relapses may occur.

ME is a physical illness with many triggers such as the Coxsackie B virus (which is the non-paralytic form of polio) and other causal factors such as chemicals within the environment (for example, organo phosphates). In the past, ME, like Multiple Sclerosis (MS), was thought by some to have been psychological in origin but this is now known to be untrue. Unfortunately, like MS, it has taken some time for medical professionals to accept ME as a physical illness and this has resulted in some parents finding themselves being told incorrectly that the illness is psychosomatic (all in the mind). Such parents are then offered therapies that are no longer regarded as appropriate for the bulk of those who have ME. (Graduated Movement therapy has been shown to cause a marked deterioration in many students and Behaviour Cognitive Therapy, favoured by some psychiatrists has been shown to have limited use or even, in some cases, to worsen the situation.)

Parents need to be aware that some professionals will know a great deal about this condition and others will know nothing. Even within the same local education/medical authority, parents may receive very different treatment. (Some children have been taken into care or hospitalised against their parent's wishes, which results in the parents losing their trust in professionals.) Some professionals may accuse the parents of keeping their children off school without good reason. Parents threatened/ pressurised by ill-informed social workers and educational/ medical professionals should contact Action for ME for advice (Tel: 01749 670799).

Due to changes within the brain chemistry of the student there is often a period of insomnia where the person has great difficulties in getting to sleep. Sleeping patterns are greatly disturbed causing the student to have problems with coping with early morning lessons. (It can take the student some time to come round in the morning; for example, two or more hours).

Flu-like symptoms are common in ME. Many types of pain may be present; for example, muscle aches, stomach migraines and headaches. All of these can be exceptionally painful and may not respond to normal painkillers.

The Specific Learning Difficulties Profile and associated conditions by Jan Poustie   ISBN 1 901544 08 7

Case study: Sophie

One father, facing significant opposition to his seven-year-old child having the time off school that she needed, corresponded in detail with the professionals involved and kept a written record of all correspondence. He was threatened with being taken to court on the grounds that, by keeping her at home, he was causing Sophie psychological damage due to missing her school friends. It was an exceptionally stressful time for him as his daughter was very ill. In the end the professionals backed off, his daughter was enabled to have the rest she needed, and her condition has now been stable for some time. Her father says,

I needed the medical and social services professionals to be understanding and give direction in managing the illness. Instead, I found that they would not listen and they were fixed in their views. I felt that they knew hardly anything about the illness and its effects upon children. I feel very bitter, I have no trust in medical and social service professionals now. I regard them as a threat rather than a support. Unfortunately, the attitude of the educational professionals was influenced by the views of the medical/social services professionals which made the whole situation worse. Thanks to my daughter's ME my life is on hold because all the personal, business and family goals have been severely limited. Many of the things that I have wanted to do with my children are either impossible, or very restricted, as my daughter uses a wheelchair and becomes fatigued so quickly. Family outings are now rare as Sophie needs so much rest and our activities have changed from outdoor ones to indoor ones. For us the care demands have been so great that only one of us can work (and that has to be part time) so the income has become greatly reduced, which affects the whole family.

We were lucky. On the same day that we received the diagnosis we happened to talk to Jan Poustie. We sourced huge amounts of information on ME plus received a lot of support from the Tymes Trust (Tel: 01245 263482) and from several ME specialists. If it had not been for all of this support (and the knowledge that we gained) we would never have survived this traumatic experience.

<u>The need for high levels of care and rest</u>

A tremendous amount of care (even twenty-four-hour care) may be necessary in the early stages of the illness . Relapses occur, especially when the child is stressed (such as when transferring to another school) and care must be taken at that time so that the child does not tire him/herself out by walking to school. Participating in PE lessons may not be possible for some time, even for those who have progressed to attending school part time. (Note: ME children should not be sent on errands instead of doing PE, as any physical exercise can be too tiring for them.)

'Children experience the symptoms of ME to a worse degree than adults, but thankfully they do have a better chance of recovery.' (Chris Clark, Chief Executive, Action for ME, AfME). Parents may need to feed, wash and dress (and act as a companion for) the child, who, especially if the condition is severe, may become increasingly isolated from the world. The student may need to rest after watching television for only half an hour. It is important to note that mental, physical and emotional activities will cause the symptoms of ME to worsen, so great care must be taken to balance the amount of activity and rest.

Case study: Lee

Lee became ill with ME in 1995 when he was six years old. He, like many others at his school, caught a viral infection in the summer term. He appeared to recover but his mother realised something was wrong when Lee, who had been able to swim 800 metres prior to his illness, was suddenly unable to swim the width of a pool. His eyes were painful and he had a continuous headache which lasted for two-and-a-half years. In Year 2, he was very tearful in class, had lots of little infections and swollen glands (indicating that he was constantly fighting an infection). Similarly his body ached continuously. The GP arranged for some blood tests, which came back 'all clear'. He was referred to a paediatrician, more blood tests were conducted (e.g. for rheumatoid arthritis), which were all negative. It was concluded that Lee had PVFS.

Lee's teacher had seen an article on PVFS and so was able to provide the appropriate provision he needed. He therefore attended school part time and when he was tired he was sent home. Lee's workload and the level of his work were reduced so that he only did essential work. The school was very sympathetic and supportive to Lee and his needs. His mother felt that this made a huge difference to them both. His friends accepted that he was ill which also made it easier for Lee. By Year 6, Lee appeared to be almost fully recovered, had an above average attendance record and, by playing in goal, (a position that requires less use of energy) he had been able to join a football team. Lee found the move from primary to secondary school very stressful although he made friends very easily. He started to have frequent illnesses and his energy levels decreased. The secondary school was very sympathetic and allowed him to go home whenever he needed to. Now, to save energy, his mother takes him to school. Despite all this, Lee has managed to keep his place in the football team, but he is excused playing when he is too tired.

Case study: Bethany

Two years older than Lee, Bethany attended the same school and had the same teacher but received a very different response.

➼ She started to talk at five months of age

➼ She developed eczema and asthma at three years of age.

➼ She watched Open University science programmes, did mathematics work two years ahead of her age, and her bedtime story came from the David Macaulay's *The Way Things Work* guide to machines at five years of age!

➼ She had whooping cough at six years of age.

➼ She was diagnosed as gifted and as having Developmental Dyslexia and Occulomotor Dyspraxia at seven years of age.

The situation developed as follows:

Although it now appears that Bethany developed ME during 1995 she was unsupported by her school. The class teacher refused to believe Bethany when she complained of headaches. Making the situation worse was the fact that Bethany was finding school very stressful, as no provision was made for her specific learning difficulties. (Despite LEA professionals advising that they were valid, the school refused to accept the private reports that diagnosed Bethany's SpLD conditions.)

The Specific Learning Difficulties Profile and associated conditions by Jan Poustie   ISBN 1 901544 08 7

Wheelchairs can be obtained via the NHS through a referral from the student's GP/ paediatric consultant. A non-electric wheelchair for home use can be acquired in the same way. While waiting for a NHS wheelchair, the person can obtain a short-term loan of a non-electric wheelchair via the local Red Cross.)

Use of a wheelchair may be essential for some students with ME. This requires much more thought on the part of parents and teaching staff when planning activities and trips. Many buildings state that they have 'limited access' for the disabled when in fact hardly any of the building can be accessed via a wheelchair.

<u>1995</u>
- ▸▸ Bethany had frequent bouts of illness and constantly enlarged neck glands indicating a lowered immune function;
- ▸▸ She was referred, via her GP, to a consultant paediatrician. Blood tests showed that Bethany's immune function was at the lower end of normal.

<u>October 1996</u>
- ▸▸ She moved to a school which had an SpLD specialist and her family caught a virus. A chemically-based nit lotion was also used on all the family. (Chemicals have been implicated in causing ME.) By Christmas all the family had recovered from the virus except Bethany.

<u>Spring term 1997</u>
- ▸▸ She had another virus and became very ill (sleeping for sixteen hours a day for a week). The GP diagnosed PVFS/ME. Her school was very supportive;
- ▸▸ She attended school half time for the next two terms. Her asthma steadily worsened. It substantially improved during a holiday in the Swiss mountains but she was so exhausted that she had to use wheelchair. On her return to the UK, she was still very tired and so a wheelchair was borrowed from the Red Cross and then she acquired the use of one permanently through her GP.

<u>Autumn term 1997</u>
- ▸▸ The family's car was 'written off'. Bethany 's school was several miles away but the LEA refused to provide transport for her even though travelling to school by public transport required a lot of walking plus taking two buses each way. As this would have exhausted her, she was off school for approximately two weeks while another car was purchased.

<u>November 1997</u>
- ▸▸ Despite her condition further deteriorating, Bethany was refused Disability Living Allowance (DLA).
- ▸▸ She had become very ill, could not support her body in a sitting position, was intolerant to noise and light, and was in considerable pain (which painkillers did little for);
- ▸▸ She could only watch television/read for a few minutes at a time due to visual difficulties;
- ▸▸ She developed severe temperature fluctuations, hot sweats that could last much of the night, and a very distorted sleeping pattern. She and her mother had little sleep during this time;
- ▸▸ She was often in severe pain day and night due to developing stomach migraines and Irritable Bowel Syndrome. Many of her SpLD difficulties had previously been overcome but now they returned, her spelling was often poor, her arithmetic

weak and her memory was muddled. She often had days when she relapsed. Her mother provided twenty-four hour care, and also used Dr Darrel Ho-Yen's methods to improve Bethany's functioning. Blood tests showed that Bethany was still fighting a viral infection, and that hypothyroidism was not present (the latter shares many symptoms with ME).

Action for ME (AfME) Conference 1997

▸ Bethany's mother found out that Bethany was entitled to an LEA tutor.

Spring/Summer terms 1998

▸ She received tuition for five hours a week via an LEA home tutor who had specialist knowledge of Dyslexia;

▸ She then attended school for one hour (four days a week) whilst having the LEA tutor for two to five hours a week;

▸ She was assessed by an LEA educational psychologist (EP) and by a community paediatrician (CP).

▸ She transferred to secondary school in September. One school refused to accept anyone on a reduced curriculum. LEA staff tried to persuade the parents to place Bethany in a school that had wheelchair access but a low academic record. A school with a good academic record accepted her (but no ramps were put in due to lack of funds).

The parents' requested a multi-disciplinary meeting, which was attended by the EP, the CP, the secondary and primary school staff, the LEA tutor and the parents. Background information on ME was provided by the parents for the EP and the secondary-school staff so that an informed decision could be made. It was agreed that Bethany should attend the secondary school for one lesson a day for four days of the week on a very reduced curriculum. An electric wheelchair was provided by the NHS for use in school and the LEA agreed to provide her with medical transport to school and to continue the home tutoring.

Autumn term 1998/present time

▸ She found the Year-7 science far too easy even though she had not studied science for two years. The AfME conference had recommended that bright children with ME take at least one of their GCCEs a year early to reduce the pressure on them in their final year. So, the parents persuaded the school to let Bethany work at a higher level;

▸ She joined the Year 9 science lessons when she was in Year 8. She started her GCSE Science one year early. She has already obtained an A and an A* for the first two modules;

▸ She now only studies three subjects; science (at school) and mathematics and English (with her LEA tutor).

Every cloud has a silver lining. Over the next two years, on the one day a week that Bethany did not attend school, she was encouraged to read. This gave her an opportunity that few of those who have Dyslexia ever have. She had the chance to spend a lot of time reading something that she wanted to read. (Many dyslexic students are too tired at the end of the school day to read for pleasure.) By age eleven, Bethany was reading the *adult* 'Star Wars' novels with ease.

Andrea's advice is:

If you do not manage this illness properly at the start you run the risk of developing a chronic form of it. It is important to rest and create a balance between your activities. Society's idea of rest is 'not working'. When PVFS is present, the person may find even common leisure activities very tiring, such as a telephone conversation, watching television, reading, going on holiday. For us, 'rest' means a complete rest from all sensory input.

Case study: Andrea

Adults too can have ME. Andrea was diagnosed early as having PVFS in a very active viral infection, which lasted about four months. PVFS caused frequent episodes of illness, which required her to be off work and in the end her GP said that the only way she was going to get better was to stop work. Since that time she has had several relapses. She was able to take on some voluntary work for a short time but her illness forced her to leave a college course. Andrea had huge swings in her functioning. She could go for several days feeling quite good and then would have several days where she could do little else but stay in bed. However, like so many with this illness, she found that 'pushing herself' was not the solution, as it only made her worse and in fact resulted in the illness becoming chronic. She therefore functions now at a low level all of the time.

Since the NHS can offer so little for ME patients, both Andrea and Bethany use various complementary treatments. Bethany has used homeopathy, aromatherapy, Bowen Treatment and magnotherapy – each of which has helped to stabilise her condition. Her occulomotor difficulties (which had been largely resolved before her November 1997 relapse) re-emerge at intervals and have required behavioural optometry intervention and the use of bifocal spectacles. As none of these interventions are available under the NHS, it became essential to obtain a Disability Living Allowance (DLA) but both Andrea and Bethany had been refused this. Bethany's family and Andrea had to go through the very stressful process of appealing against this decision (which includes being examined by a DLA-appointed doctor). The doctor recommended Graded Aerobic Exercise for Bethany but her parents realised the damage that this could cause and so refused it. The effort of applying for a DLA caused Andrea to relapse for several months. Thanks to the support of The Orchard Centre for Fatigue Illnesses (Tel: 01902 49471) the cases went to the Disability Appeal Tribunal and were awarded DLA at the High Mobility rate plus care. Bethany was awarded DLA nearly two-and-a-half years after being diagnosed as having PVFS whilst Andrea was awarded it after having PVFS for eight years (including being chronically ill for five years).

Recommended reading

📖 *ME Post-Viral Fatigue Syndrome: How to Live With It* by Dr Anne Macintyre (ISBN 0 7225 2624 5). Written by a medical doctor who has the condition. Contains checklists of the symptoms of ME

📖 *ME: the New Plague* by Jane Colby (ISBN 1 8608 3215 6 Published by First & Best in Education.) Written by an ex-headteacher who has the condition.

📖 *Better recovery from viral illnesses* by Dr Darrel Ho-Yen (ISBN 0 951109 03 0, published by Dodona Books). An excellent book. It enables one to devise a plan that helps the individual to either recover from ME or to stabilise the condition.

📖 *Somebody help ME* by Jill I Moss (ISBN 0 9525 783 01, published by Sunbow Books). A self-help guide for young people who have Myalgic Encephalomyelitis and their families.

Help and Support

CFS/ME
ME Association
Stanhope House, High Street, Stanford-le-Hope,
Essex, SS17 0HA   Tel: 01375 642466

Action for ME
P.O. Box 1302, Wells, BA5 2WE
Tel: 01749 670799

Action for Young ME
Website: www.ayme.org.uk

CHILDHOOD HEMIPLEGIA
Hemihelp
166 Boundaries Road, London, SW12 8EG
Tel: 020 8672 3179
Offers help to parents and professionals. Produces a newsletter.
Helpline: Mon–Fri, 10am–1pm.

Child Head Injury Trust
Mrs Sue Colville (secretary), The Children's Head Injury Trust,
c/o Neurosurgery Department, The Radcliffe Infirmary,
Woodstock Road, Oxford, OX2 6HE.

(continued overleaf)

The Specific Learning Difficulties Profile and associated conditions by Jan Poustie   ISBN 1 901544 08 7

OTHER CONDITIONS

The Fragile X Society

53 Winchelsea Lane, Hastings, East Sussex, TN35 4LG
Tel: 01424 813147. Email: info@fragilex.k-web.co.uk
Website: http://www.fragilex.org.uk/
Supports families and provides information, including the latest medical and educational research findings. Provides (free to families and individual professional enquirers) an *Introductory Fragile X Information* pack which includes the booklet *Fragile X Syndrome: An Introduction to Education Needs*. The latter includes information on speech and language, behaviour, numeracy and literacy. The Society has a twenty minute documentary video called *Fragile X Syndrome* (costing £5 inc. p & p) which explains the features and behaviours of Fragile X, its genetics and its inheritance patterns. It also discusses the benefits and implications of diagnosis and gives examples of intervention and teaching strategies

National Asthma Campaign

Providence House, Providence Place, London, N1 0NT,
Tel. 0207 226 2260;
Asthma Helpline: 08457 010203 (9am-7pm, Monday-Friday),
Fax: 0207 7040740, Website: www.asthma.org.uk
Provides information, including a large number of very useful free leaflets including *Asthma at School*.

National Eczema Society

Hill House, Highgate Hill, London, N19 5NA,
el. 0207 2813553, Helpline: 0870 2413604,
Website: www.eczema.org
Provides numerous, very useful free leaflets.

CHAPTER 3
Finding out the views of the student

In order to provide appropriate and effective provision we need to find out the views of the student with regard to his/her provision and his/her progress.

Finding out the views of the student

It is common to consult with, and find out, the views of the parents/affected adult/teachers when deciding upon provision but often the student's viewpoint is either not considered or given too little consideration. The government's 'Code of Practice on the Identification and Assessment of Special Educational Needs' (due 2002) regards it as essential that the student's point of view is taken into consideration when planning provision. All too often this is not the case simply because people do not know how to find out the views of the child (especially if s/he is very young). The solution to this problem is to use the 'Worry Clouds' sheets (explained below) which are easily administered and make it simple to check on the effectiveness of provision from the child's point of view. Ideally this method should be used at least once a term, preferably twice a term during the early stages of provision. It is sometimes useful to ask the teacher/therapist/parent also to fill in one of the Worry Cloud sheets in order to ascertain their view of the student's needs. The child's concerns may be very different from those of the adult. It is the child who is being provided for, so it is essential that we meet his or her needs; not just those that we think s/he ought to have!

Using the Worry Clouds sheets

Worry cloud sheets can be found in Appendix 1. The first sheet covers main areas of possible difficulty. With some children, adults may prefer to use this page followed by the last page. (By the time the child has filled in the first page s/he will usually want to tell the adult what his/her other worries are.) However, if there is a language impairment or the child is anxious, using the first three pages, which are all picture-based may be a better idea. The first line of the clouds on page one is blank – these are the 'Things I am good' at clouds. Spend some time discussing these things first. This will put the child at ease and allow use of the child's strengths to improve areas of weakness when designing the programme of provision. Each student will need the following:

A   Three different coloured pens/felt-tips/wax crayons (for example, e.g. yellow, purple, and green) – whatever is appropriate for the student's age. (Avoid having both red

Reading

The use of the WORRY CLOUDS strategy is very useful when assessing appropriate provision for children. To a child, the little things matter. S/he may be more disturbed at sitting next to someone who keeps teasing him/her than finding writing difficult. Yes, the writing will need to be attended to but the child's environment can be made much happier if his/her neighbour is moved to another position within the classroom.

It does not matter what is put into the 'Things I am good at' clouds; e.g. making my friends laugh, stroking the cat etc. We want the child to see that there are some things that s/he can do! Some children are good at very unusual things; e.g. the secondary-school child who was good at 'Counting ants'!!

Comparison between the child's response to numbers 4 and 5 gives us some useful information. It may be that the student is only worried about something before s/he goes to school and is fine once in school – this can put the parent's mind at rest. Some children will draw a large cross to indicate a major worry, or lots of crosses in the cloud if it is a real problem area.

and green, as it is one of the commonest colour-blind combinations. Avoid wax crayons if Dyspraxia is thought to be present, as the student may dislike the feel of the wax.)

B   The Worry Clouds sheets

1.   Using the top three clouds (Things I am good at), record what the child feels that s/he is good at.

2.   Point to the next section on the sheet (My Worry Clouds). Explain to the child that sometimes we worry over things. The assessor should point to the picture and read the words as follows (using reading as the chosen task):

3.   'In a minute I am going to ask you to draw on a piece of paper to show me how you feel about the things you do in school. We will look at reading at first'

4.   The child is shown three pens. The adult says the following (whilst pointing to the appropriate colour) to ensure that the child knows what to do.

   ▸ 'Use the yellow pen and draw a sun if you are not worried about your reading.'

   ▸ 'Use the green pen if you are only worried a little bit about your reading.'

   ▸ 'Use the purple pen if reading is a middle-sized worry.'

   ▸ 'Use the black pen if reading is a big worry.'

5.   The adult then asks: 'Before you go to school are your worried about your reading?' If the child replies no, then the adult draws a sun beside the cloud and explains the sun shows that the student is not worried about this task.
      If the child answers 'yes', the adult says: 'We are going to draw a line underneath the reading picture'. The adult then points to the cloud and helps the child to select the appropriate coloured pen, by saying, for example, 'If this is a little worry before you go to school, we will use the green pen'. The adult then gives the selected pen to the child and asks him/ her to draw a line beneath the cloud. (The adult should show the child how to do it.)

6.   The adult now tells the child that we are looking at reading once s/he gets to school (e.g. 'When you are at school, is reading a little worry?' etc.). This time the child draws a cross or a circle over the cloud (or another shape that s/he finds easy to draw).

7.   Do the same with all of the clouds, make sure that the procedure above is followed to ensure that the child uses the colour that reflects his/her feelings.

When working with children under seven years, the tutor/parent may want to do this exercise twice (with a least a few days between each one) to ensure reliability. There may also be need to repeat stage number 4 before going on to number 5 to make sure that the student makes the right choice of pen.

<u>Finding out the views of the older child/adult</u>
The 'How I Feel' sheets (pages 37-39) can be used from the age of about ten years onwards (though some younger children will prefer to use them rather than the Worry Clouds.) By the age of ten the individual is conditioned to thinking in tens, since much of his/her school work will have been marked out of ten. In this sheet the child is grading him/herself out of ten against his/her peer group. Again, if the professionals (and the parent if appropriate) also fill in the sheets some interesting results emerge, as we find out the concerns of each of the adults as compared with the student. The final How I Feel sheets contain spare sets of numbers, which can have headings added to them as appropriate. As a rule of thumb, anything graded five or below needs immediate provision, the lower the number, the greater the need for provision. The long-term aim of the provision is, whenever possible, to enable the student to function at the eight, nine or ten level for all skills.

Student's needs versus the professional's/parent's wants
Sometimes the child/affected adult will be totally happy with some (or all) aspects of his/her functioning (e.g. literacy skills) even though the professionals/parents are not. The professionals/parents want to help the student but s/he has a different agenda and/or is prioritising his/her needs in a different way. If, initially, there is a concentration on providing for the areas that concern the student, this will boost self-confidence and self-esteem and often will have a 'knock-on' effect on his/her literacy and numeracy skills. It may also lead to a decrease in inappropriate behaviours of those with Attention Deficits etc. Once the person is happier s/he may more readily accept help in the areas of difficulty where the professional/parent knows it is needed.

Stress
All of the conditions found within the SpLD Profile seem to have one thing in common; namely, difficulties in the perception of certain areas of information, and in the classification, planning and organisation of information and its prioritisation. (See *Planning and Organisation Solutions* by Jan Poustie, ISBN 1 901544 818, for details of how to help students with such difficulties.) Individuals may also have difficulties in making decisions, which can range from a mild to a severe problem. The less severely affected may have problems

When working in the field of Specific Learning Difficulties the saying -'You can take a horse to water but you cannot make it drink' is especially appropriate. However, there is fortunately more than 'one way to skin a cat!' The innovative teacher/therapist may be able to 'slip in' elements of the necessary tuition whilst supplying the provision that the student wants.

Both the Worry Clouds and the How I Feel sheets can be used to review the student's progress at half-termly intervals, and to enable the focus of provision to alter as frequently as necessary.

The Specific Learning Difficulties Profile and associated conditions by Jan Poustie   ISBN 1 901544 08 7

Those with severe difficulties may not be able to decide what to eat from the fridge or which colour of paper to write on.

Stress increases the body's demands for a number of nutrients, which, if they are not supplied, lead to a person becoming fatigued and ill. Adelle Davis in *Let's get well* (ISBN 0 7225 27101-2) recommends taking an anti-stress formula at least three times a day at times of severe stress (e.g. during GCSE examinations) whilst also following an anti-stress diet. The formula for adults consists of 500 mg of vitamin C, 100 mg of panothenic acid and at least 2 mg each of vitamins B6 and B2, taken with protein (e.g. a glass of milk).

deciding issues such as the criteria that are important to them when choosing a new house to live in. It should be noted that individuals whose learning difficulties remain unidentified and unprovided for are likely to be under stress. The longer the situation has existed, the greater the stress. The majority of SpLD Profile students (or those who have the conditions which can be seen alongside the Profile) are likely to be under stress in the academic environment. The more stress the individual is under, the greater the difficulties with planning, organisation and decision making. Stress will also affect the functioning of the brain and is likely to cause the individual to cope less well with handling and interpreting symbolic information such as letters, numerals and musical notation. Once the person has become severely stressed (e.g. due to his/her needs not being met in the academic environment) then even the long summer holidays are not long enough to reduce the stress to acceptable levels. Remember such stress can apply to both students and teachers/LSAs!

The greater the stress the more likely also that the student's eating and sleeping patterns will be affected. Stressed students need to feel emotionally satisfied when doing a task and intervention is likely to be less effective unless this occurs. Thus these students will need to have a pleasant association with the material to be learned and the professional providing the tuition. The best way to achieve this is for the task to be modified to suit the student's interests, or, at least, introduced in a way that relates to his/her interests. Students of all ages can become interested in the task if it relates to their hobbies and will often cope with an advanced text in such cases. Suiting the method of tuition to the student's natural learning style will also make tuition more meaningful and effective.

Once we know that stress affects the neo-cortex area of the brain (which deals with symbolic information) it becomes easier to view both Dyscalculia and Dyslexia as indicating the presence of other developmental conditions rather than necessarily being the main causal conditions behind the learning difficulties. Identification of all conditions present is essential if appropriate and effective provision is to be made. Armed with an identification (leading to diagnosis) plus an understanding of the way the condition/s affect learning we can reduce the stress within the learning process, the learning environment and the task through remediating the problems at the foundation level of learning and by amending the diet to reduce the effects of stress. Only then can we ease the effects of the SpLD Profile conditions upon the student's learning, behaviour and language.

APPENDIX 1
Student Report Forms

Guidance for using the Student Report Forms

For overall instructions please read pages 27 and 28.

Writing Notes in the report forms:
Spaces have been allocated for notes on the factors that make it more difficult for the student to perform a particular task; for example:

➤ when writing, the student may find that the elbow of the left-handed student sitting at the same table is knocking into him/her.

➤ the noise from a nearby radiator may be distracting the student.

➤ the student may dislike one of the reading schemes in the classroom.

➤ SpLD students are often bullied, which can make the student so stressed that s/he has greater difficulties in learning and is unhappy at school.

The Specific Learning Difficulties Profile and associated conditions by Jan Poustie   ISBN 1 901544 08 7

Student Report Form: WORRY CLOUDS

Name: **Date:**   **Class:**

Things I am good at:

I have problems with:

reading

spelling

c a t

number

Notes:

writing and drawing

writing my thoughts

being messy

Notes:

The Specific Learning Difficulties Profile and associated conditions by Jan Poustie   ISBN 1 901544 08 7

The Specific Learning Difficulties Profile and associated conditions by Jan Poustie   ISBN 1 901544 08 7

mental
arithmetic

3+2:5

not knowing
my tables

1 x 2 = 2
2 x 2 = 4
3 x 2 = 6

drawing
shapes

Notes:

using a ruler

sums

2 + 4 = 6   1 x 3 = 3

8 – 1 = 7   4 ÷ 2 = 2

children in my
class

Notes:

getting
dressed

P E

Notes:

The Specific Learning Difficulties Profile and associated conditions by Jan Poustie   ISBN 1 901544 08 7

Notes:

Notes:

Notes:

The Specific Learning Difficulties Profile and associated conditions by Jan Poustie   ISBN 1 901544 08 7

Student Report Form: HOW I FEEL

Name

....

Date ....
Class ....

 0 = Very little (or no) skill in this area.
10 = Usual functioning of peer group.

Put a circle round the number that shows how well you can do each activity.

I am good (or okay) at:
(Can include any activities, hobbies, sports and so on, as well any area of the curriculum)

Notes:

0   1   2   3   4   5   6   7   8   9   10   ....

0   1   2   3   4   5   6   7   8   9   10   ....

0   1   2   3   4   5   6   7   8   9   10   ....

I have some difficulty with:
NUMBERS

0   1   2   3   4   5   6   7   8   9   10   ....

TABLES 2 X, 5 X AND 10 X

0   1   2   3   4   5   6   7   8   9   10   ....

TABLES 3 X AND 4 X

0   1   2   3   4   5   6   7   8   9   10   ....

TABLES 6 X , 7 X, 8 X AND 9 X

0   1   2   3   4   5   6   7   8   9   10   ....

Continued overleaf.

The Specific Learning Difficulties Profile and associated conditions by Jan Poustie   ISBN 1 901544 08 7

Notes:

…..………………...……..

WORKING AT SPEED IN MATHS

0   1   2   3   4   5   6   7   8   9   10

…………………...……..

READING (understanding what I have read)

0   1   2   3   4   5   6   7   8   9   10

………………….....……..

WORKING AT SPEED IN ENGLISH

0   1   2   3   4   5   6   7   8   9   10

…………………...……..

WORKING AT SPEED WHEN I AM READING

0   1   2   3   4   5   6   7   8   9   10

WORD FINDING
(Not being able to remember the word I want to use)

0   1   2   3   4   5   6   7   8   9   10

…………………...……..

WORD LABELLING
(Not being able to remember the names of things and symbols)

0   1   2   3   4   5   6   7   8   9   10

…………………...……..

WRITING (Putting my thoughts down on paper)

0   1   2   3   4   5   6   7   8   9   10

…………………...……..

PLANNING AND ORGANISATION
(of myself, my work, my desk, my bag, my room)

0   1   2   3   4   5   6   7   8   9   10

…………………...……..

SELF-ESTEEM (How I feel about myself)

0   1   2   3   4   5   6   7   8   9   10

…………………...……..

HANDWRITING
0   1   2   3   4   5   6   7   8   9   10

…………………………...

The Specific Learning Difficulties Profile and associated conditions by Jan Poustie   ISBN 1 901544 08 7

THINKING

| 0 | 1 | 2 | 3 | 4 | 5 | 6 | 7 | 8 | 9 | 10 |

Notes:

....

LISTENING (following instructions)

| 0 | 1 | 2 | 3 | 4 | 5 | 6 | 7 | 8 | 9 | 10 |

....

UNDERSTANDING (what my teacher says)

| 0 | 1 | 2 | 3 | 4 | 5 | 6 | 7 | 8 | 9 | 10 |

....

| 0 | 1 | 2 | 3 | 4 | 5 | 6 | 7 | 8 | 9 | 10 |

....

| 0 | 1 | 2 | 3 | 4 | 5 | 6 | 7 | 8 | 9 | 10 |

....

AREAS I WOULD LIKE TO IMPROVE
0 = I am not very good at this
10 = I am very good at this

| 0 | 1 | 2 | 3 | 4 | 5 | 6 | 7 | 8 | 9 | 10 |

....

| 0 | 1 | 2 | 3 | 4 | 5 | 6 | 7 | 8 | 9 | 10 |

....

| 0 | 1 | 2 | 3 | 4 | 5 | 6 | 7 | 8 | 9 | 10 |

....

| 0 | 1 | 2 | 3 | 4 | 5 | 6 | 7 | 8 | 9 | 10 |

....

| 0 | 1 | 2 | 3 | 4 | 5 | 6 | 7 | 8 | 9 | 10 |

....

The Specific Learning Difficulties Profile and associated conditions by Jan Poustie   ISBN 1 901544 08 7

General Index

The Specific Learning Difficulties Profile and associated conditions by Jan Poustie   ISBN 1 901544 08 7

Resource Index

The Specific Learning Difficulties Profile and associated conditions by Jan Poustie   ISBN 1 901544 08 7